Norwegian Forest Cats as Pets

A Pet Guide for Norwegian Forest Cats

Norwegian Forest Cats General Info, Purchasing, Care, Cost, Keeping, Health, Supplies, Food, Breeding and More Included!

By Lolly Brown

Copyrights and Trademarks

All rights reserved. No part of this book may be reproduced or transformed in any form or by any means, graphic, electronic, or mechanical, including photocopying, recording, taping, or by any information storage retrieval system, without the written permission of the author.

This publication is Copyright ©2018 NRB Publishing, an imprint. Nevada. All products, graphics, publications, software and services mentioned and recommended in this publication are protected by trademarks. In such instance, all trademarks & copyright belong to the respective owners. For information consult www.NRBpublishing.com

Disclaimer and Legal Notice

This product is not legal, medical, or accounting advice and should not be interpreted in that manner. You need to do your own due-diligence to determine if the content of this product is right for you. While every attempt has been made to verify the information shared in this publication, neither the author, neither publisher, nor the affiliates assume any responsibility for errors, omissions or contrary interpretation of the subject matter herein. Any perceived slights to any specific person(s) or organization(s) are purely unintentional.

We have no control over the nature, content and availability of the web sites listed in this book. The inclusion of any web site links does not necessarily imply a recommendation or endorse the views expressed within them. We take no responsibility for, and will not be liable for, the websites being temporarily unavailable or being removed from the internet.

The accuracy and completeness of information provided herein and opinions stated herein are not guaranteed or warranted to produce any particular results, and the advice and strategies, contained herein may not be suitable for every individual. Neither the author nor the publisher shall be liable for any loss incurred as a consequence of the use and application, directly or indirectly, of any information presented in this work. This publication is designed to provide information in regard to the subject matter covered.

Neither the author nor the publisher assume any responsibility for any errors or omissions, nor do they represent or warrant that the ideas, information, actions, plans, suggestions contained in this book is in all cases accurate. It is the reader's responsibility to find advice before putting anything written in this book into practice. The information in this book is not intended to serve as legal, medical, or accounting advice.

Foreword

Cats are amazing house pets that will surely change your views about life. They are happy, little fur balls that will ensure you that there is no dull moment when you are with it. A great example of a cat is the Norwegian Forest Cat.

Say hello to the beloved cat of Norway, in this country, this breed is known as the "skogkatt," which translates to "forest cat." When it first landed to Northern America, it was given the name the "Norwegian Forest Cat," since its name was too long for anyone to mention, this breed has a nickname of "Wegie".

The Norwegian Forest Cat boasts to be a kind, gentle, and loving cat that possesses a strong nurturing instinct. The breed is surely noticeable due to its double coat of many patterns and colors, triangular head, tufted ears and paws, plumed tail, and a heavily and sturdy muscled body.

Wegie is great for people who will shower it with love and comb its coat every now and then. There are many things that we can discover about the Norwegian Forest Cat, and if you plan to own one, this guide book will surely help you! Read on and travel into the land of the Norwegian Forest Cat.

Table of Contents

Introduction 1

Chapter One: Wegie's Basic Information and Colorful History 3

    Norwegian Forest Cat's History 5

    Interesting Characteristics 7

        Quick Facts 8

Chapter Two: Why Norwegian Forest Cat is Perfect for You 11

    This Is the Greatest Cat You Will Ever Have 12

    Temperament and Behavioral Characteristics 13

    Behavioral Characteristics with other Pets 14

    Should I Get the Norwegian Forest Cat? 15

        KITTY LITTER… AND A LOT OF PATIENCE 24

        A COMFORTABLE AND LUXURIOUS BED 24

        A STURDY SCRATCHING POST 25

        WATER AND FOOD BOWLS 26

        A LOT OF TOYS 26

        GROOMING TOOLS 27

        CARRIER AND COLLAR 27

        CAT FOOD AND TREATS 28

Chapter Three: Finding the Norwegian Forest Cat Suited For You 29

    Kitten or Adult: What Shall I Choose?............................... 30

        A Rescued Cat for Your Big Heart............................... 33

    A Reputable Norwegian Forest Cat Breeder 34

    A Healthy and Happy Norwegian Forest Cat.................... 37

Chapter Four: Taking Your Norwegian Forest Cat Home .. 39

    Living Spaces for Our Norwegian Forest Cat.................... 40

        CAT BED AND BEDDING.. 41

        CARRIERS.. 42

        LITTER AND ITS LITTER BOX 42

        SCRATCHING POST 44

        CAT PROOFING 101... 44

Chapter Five: Feeding Your Norwegian Forest Cat Yummy and Nutritious Food 47

    Wants vs. Needs: What's More Important? 48

    Your Norwegian Forest Cat's Nutritional Needs.............. 48

    Choosing the Right Food for Wegie 50

    The Main Food Choices for Your Cat.................................. 51

        COMMERCIALLY MADE vs. HOMEMADE 51

        RAW MEAT vs. COOKED MEAT.................................... 52

    Kinds of Commercial Cat Food.. 52

Feeding Amount and Frequency 53

What Not To Give To Your Cat 54

Chapter Six: Time to Groom Your Norwegian Forest Cat ... 57

   Make the Grooming Task Enjoyable 58

      BRUSHING YOUR CAT'S FUR 58

      BATHING YOUR CAT 59

      CLIPPING YOUR CAT'S NAIL 60

   Tools of the Trade 61

      NAIL CLIPPERS 61

      BRUSHES JUST FOR YOUR CAT 61

      PET WIPES AND SPRAYS: A NEW WAY? 62

Chapter Seven: Tips for Showing Your Norwegian Forest Cat 63

   Point Scores in Shows 64

   The Norwegian Forest Cat Breed Standard 64

   Preparing Your Cat for the Show 68

      KNOWING THE SHOW SCHEDULE 69

      FILL OUT THE ENTRY FORM 69

      CLEAN YOUR CAT 69

Chapter Eight: Building Your Relationship with Your Cat through Training 71

   Basic Cat Training 72

    USING THE LITTER BOX 72

    TEACHING GOOD BEHAVIOR 73

    TRAIN NOT TO BE AGGRESSIVE 74

    CAN YOU REALLY NOT TRAIN YOUR CAT? 74

Five Things to Remember When I Train My Wegie 75

    I SHOULD NOT PUNISH 75

    CLICKER AND TREATS ARE MY TOOLS 75

    TEACHING YOUR CAT TO COME 76

    BE PLEASANT, SHAKE HANDS! 76

    IS IT OKAY TO BEG? 77

    WALKING ON A LEASH: ONLY A DOG'S TASK? 77

Chapter Nine: Keeping Your Norwegian Forest Cat Healthy and Safe 79

  Why Should I Vaccine My Norwegian Forest Cat? 79

    THOROUGH PHYSICAL EXAMINATION 81

    INFECTIOUS DISEASE 86

    CANCER 86

    HEARTWORM DISEASE 87

    FLEAS 88

    KIDNEY DISEASE 88

    DENTAL PROBLEMS 89

    FRACTURES 90

DIARRHEA AND VOMITING 90
OBESITY 91
The Norwegian Forest Cat in General 93
Glossary of Cat Terms 99
Index 105
Photo Credits 109
References 111

Introduction

The Norwegian Forest Cat is commonly known as the Skogkatt in this native land, Norway. This breed boasts to be a large, semi-long haired cat from the feline family. Although it may look fierce and hard, Wegie is a home cat that likes to be with other pets especially their human counterparts.

This Forest Cat is commonly known as a lap dog; this breed is also known to be independent and will decide where it goes and where it stays. They like to be near their humans but they will decide where they will stay, they could be comfortable in their desktop, chair, or even bed.

Introduction

These furry active cats have a lot of energies but then followed by long naps. They are sensitive yet social creatures that easily adapt to a change in environment. Wegie has a waterproof, insulated double coat that could stand even the hardest winter any country could give. Aside from this, the texture of the coat can also help fight off the weather, coarse, long hair that lies over a dense undercoat. Although this breed is fairly new to the United States soil, it is a very old breed in Norway, which was featured in a lot of mythology and folk tales for century. This breed was believed to help Vikings explore the ships and keep clear of rodents. This breed usually can bear kittens starting from twelve weeks of age.

There are many things, still, that you need to learn about the Norwegian Forest Cat, such as its colorful history, showing requirements, grooming rules, breeding tips and regulations, and even health concerns. These things are very important as you will not only take care of your cat for only a year, you will take care of your cat for its entire lifespan, so better give it the best care possible.

This book will help you know if the Norwegian Forest Cat fits your personality and your home. You need to read this guide book first before you go off and buy your first pet. Let us start our journey by knowing where our loving cat came from.

Chapter One: Wegie's Basic Information and Colorful History

Norwegian Forest Cats are essentially known for their fluffy coats, big builds, and socialization. They are loved by people as their home companions and known to be the things that could possible take their stress away especially after work. Although this breed has the name "FOREST" in its name, this breed loves to be cozy and comfortable at their home with their humans. Although this breed likes to be around people, do not believe that it will like being around you every time and will obey you at every command. This cat has its own volition and is not afraid to use it.

Wegie's are very selective with whom they give their affection, they choose the people who they will be close to.

Chapter One: Basic Information and Colorful History

So, if your cat is very close to you, believe that this is a huge compliment. You need to build a relationship with the cat to gain its trust, remember, having a cat is being with another living being in your life – which means it needs to be socialized often and with tender loving care.

Aside from this wonderful trait, this breed has a wonderful dense double coat that is suited for winters and is waterproof. For the Norwegian Forest Cats, the length of their coat greatly varies from the different seasons, mostly during winter. During summer and spring, the breed sheds of the extra hair because they do not need much fur during these seasons. Because of the hard winters in Norway, Wegies are really great with kids and other animals and have surpassed great changes in the environment. They can adapt to different environments easily and efficiently.

If your friends have Norwegian Forest Cat, you will know that this breed loves to be in high place. They love to perch themselves high up in a tree to intake the great view of the surrounding, and can even rest for several minutes. They are silent cat yet very observant, so you can know that they will get lost in great nature.

In the first chapter, we will be giving you the life history of this breed as well as its basic characteristics. We will also be dealing about amazing facts that you will not believe! Make sure you have a hot cup of coffee with you

Chapter One: Basic Information and Colorful History

because you will surely enjoy this chapter --- or even this whole book! Enjoy!

Norwegian Forest Cat's History

The Norwegian Forest Cat hails all the way from Norway, as the name suggests. It is believed that their history goes back to hundreds or maybe thousands of years ago!

This breed has been the topic or character in several legends of fairy tales; a notable tale which the Norwegian Forest Cat belongs to is from the story of the Norse goddess Freya. In this story, Freya, the goddess of fertility and love, drove a carriage with the help of the forest cat to Balder's funeral.

A true mystery is how or where the cat has originated. Some believe that these long hired cats are descendants from Turkey, that were with the Scandanavian warriors who have fought in the Byzantine Empire, or some even believe that they might be a family member of the Siberian cat from Russia. This breed was believed to be farm animals that usually reside outside or wherever shelter they have.

Chapter One: Basic Information and Colorful History

For several years, Wegies survived through its intelligence and even offered its services as mousers to farmers.

People have believed that this breed has evolved from various cat breeds such as the Siberian, Maine Coon, the Turkish long hairs. Historians have pointed out that these breed have the common ancestor, but this theory is still just a speculation.

It is not until 1938 that anyone from Norway thought of this breed as a special breed. The breed was further defamed during the World War II, wherein Wegie was almost forgotten until the 1970s.

In 1975, the Norsk Skogkattrig, the Norwegian Forest Cat Club, was established by the Norwegian cat breeders in order to prolong the lifespan of this breed, where it was formally recognized by the Federation International Feline (FIFe).

The first pair of Norwegian Forest Cat arrived in the states in 1978. In 1987, the breed was included in the CFA's breed catalog.

Chapter One: Basic Information and Colorful History

Interesting Characteristics

There are several things you need to know about this breed. Here are some interesting facts we believe you need to know if you ever think of purchasing one. These things are somehow not present in other cat breeds, make sure you look at the cat pros and compare it with other cat breeds!

The Name Does Not Really Define the Breeders

Although the breed is called "Norwegian Forest Cat", this breed does not really mind if it needs to stay indoors, or even staying on a couch near its human. If you think that your cat will cling on you because you are its human, you are probably wrong. This cat will not be your typical lap cat. They select whom they trust and also whom they choose to be close with.

It loves to play and stay wherever it can. So, you should not confine it in a specific area, make it free and run wild in your house and backyard.

They are Technically Waterproof

They have this dense double coat that helps them keep warm during winter, especially in their native region. For the Norwegian Forest Cat, their coat will vary in

Chapter One: Basic Information and Colorful History

different seasons. They shed off excess fur during summer months as they do not need this extra hair during this season.

What a good thing right? You do not need to worry about your cat being too hot during summer and being too cold during the winter season – the cat does the thing for you!

They are 'Chill'

This breed boasts to be 'chill'. They love to be with kids and other animals but can still chill wherever it can, and they remain calm throughout the day.

They can be often seen with a calm face while observing anything that is happening around them. They love to look at their humans, especially from up above.

Quick Facts

Origin: Norway

Breed Size: medium size

Body Type and Appearance: they have a well-balanced body structure, with great emerald green eyes (with specks of gold), and an equilateral triangular shape of a head.

Chapter One: Basic Information and Colorful History

Height: 48 inches (122 cm)

Weight: 22 lbs (10 kg)

Group: Longhair

Coat Length: double coat, dense and long

Coat Texture: smooth and firm

Color: golden, fawn, black, brown, white

Temperament: kind, gentle, loving, cat with a strong nurturing instinct.

Strangers: they hide under furniture or even hide in another room

Other Cats: gets along well with other cat

Other Pets: they are friendly with other pets

Health Conditions: generally healthy but may contract several diseases such as hip dysplasia, glycogen storage disease, and hypertrophic cardiomyopathy.

Lifespan: average 12 to 16 years

Here is the basic information about our beloved Norwegian Forest Cat. You need to know these things as somehow a friendly introduction about this exotic breed. However, there are a lot to learn more. These are just some of the essential things that you need to know about our dearest Norwegian Forest Cat. However, we are only scratching the surface of the wonderful world of this breed.

Chapter One: Basic Information and Colorful History

Let us go further and know the inner world of this fantastic breed. Make sure you have your pens ready and be sure to take down some notes!

Chapter Two: Why Norwegian Forest Cat is Perfect for You

The basic information about the Norwegian Forest Cat is not enough for you to decide whether you really need to buy this breed as your own companion, there are a lot of things you still need to know about this fantastic little fur balls. Norwegian Forest Cats are notoriously known as sole survivors. They can be their own bosses but still remain perfectly calm in any situation. If you think this kind of cat suits you, then let's get it on! However, if you are still undecided whether you want to keep this as pet, you still need to read on and know more about this breed, because

Chapter Two: Why Norwegian Forest Cat is Perfect for You

you never know – you might want a Norwegian Forest Cat in the future.

This section will deal on why the Norwegian Forest Cat is the best for you, we will be highlighting its pros and cons as well as the things you need to have prior to having the cat at home. Let us read on and know if the breed is just right for you.

This Is the Greatest Cat You Will Ever Have

The first pet you will ever buy will be the biggest decision you will ever do. There are certain things that you need to consider before you even step out and buy the pet. If you ever want to buy a cat, the Norwegian Forest Cat is a good choice for you.

The Norwegian Forest Cat is the pride and glory of Norway, where it is known to be a majestic cat that will surpass any weather condition due to its durable and trustworthy double coat. If you think taking care of a cat is that easy, you are probably wrong.

There are a lot of things that you need to know about this cat, such as its temperament around humans and other pets, grooming needs, training standards, show standards, and more.

Chapter Two: Why Norwegian Forest Cat is Perfect for You

A great thing about this breed is this history, there are several tales featuring this cat. Who would not want a famous cat as their pet? In this chapter, we will go in one by one and discuss why this cat is perfectly suited for you.

Temperament and Behavioral Characteristics

Although it has the 'forest' in its name, Wegie is not really that feral. This breed loves people, but does not really show it off. It will not ask for attention, unless you give the meals late, if this case happens, it will follow you everywhere and hang out wherever you are staying,

The Norwegian Forest Cat has a mellow attitude that makes it a perfect fit with families, especially those with children and other pets. Your cat will be comfortable in your family if you have raised it well. Make sure that your children the cat gently and with great respect that it needs.

It has an average energy level, not too active but not that lazy either. Just like any other cats, it appreciates having a great and high cat tree on which it will perch for long hours. Its great agility and strength will make it capable of scaling great heights without any effort.

A great thing about this breed is that it is not too vocal or loud, but will speak to you using soft meows and chirps. Wegies enjoy attention and smart especially during

Chapter Two: Why Norwegian Forest Cat is Perfect for You

training sessions. You can challenge its brain through teaching him tricks and providing with toys, but do not forget to reward it with treats or kibbles, only when it learns to manipulate the thing.

Behavioral Characteristics with other Pets

Norwegian Forest Cat is great with other cat breed, however, it may need some time to interact and get comfortable with other pets.

If your cat is already well versed with the other cats and breeds inside your house, your cat will surely enjoy the company it can get. It will not really mind if it is not the only pet in the house, rather, it will enjoy having someone to keep as a company and friend.

You may need to supervise the initial meeting of your old pet with the Norwegian Forest Cat, to ensure that they will not fit and get along well.

Chapter Two: Why Norwegian Forest Cat is Perfect for You

Should I Get the Norwegian Forest Cat?

Buying a cat is a big decision; it will entail bringing up another creature in your life and taking care of it for a long time. However, this could be a great companion especially if you live alone, or just fond of animals. The Norwegian Forest Cat is a great choice as a pet, however, the breed is not really known and they might not be seen as opposed to the famous tabbies.

In this part, we will be listing down the positive and negative traits about the Norwegian Forest Cat. Make sure you weigh the pros with the cons before you finally choose if you want to buy this breed.

What's Good about Them?

- They are easily adaptable.

This cat easily adapts to change wherever it is. This breed is open to any changes in their life. The Norwegian Forest Cat will enjoy their life whoever they are spending it with. If you are out of town, the cat will not panic if you will let other people take care of it. They are totally chill with whatever happens inside their house, they are very independent.

Chapter Two: Why Norwegian Forest Cat is Perfect for You

- Wegies Love Children

Cats are notoriously known as aloof and unfriendly, especially when it comes to the little ones. However, you as a fur parent and if you have children, you would want that both of your children would get along together. Norwegian Forest Cat loves kids! Wegies love to play with kids, spend their free time with them, and knows how to deal with it even if they get too handsy. Another plus for this breed, they will not get too aggressive with them in case they get too aggressive with them. This is a major pro for this breed; you need to choose a cat that will love every member of the family.

- They Are So Fluffy

Cats are naturally fluffy with long hair, which makes them so beautiful. A downside of this trait is that cat hair will be everywhere! You can find hair on the couch, floor, or even in the air! Norwegian Forest Cat, however, is not the same. It has a long coat, but its coat does not require too much grooming, nor do they have too much shedding. You may just need to brush every three or four days to make sure you get the excess hair.

Chapter Two: Why Norwegian Forest Cat is Perfect for You

- They Are Smarty Pants

Norwegian Forest Cats are intelligent. They love adults, kids, and even instructions. This breed loves to follow instructions and knows how to do things right, so you will not think that they might break the rules. Just give a strong no for a couple of times and it will learn not to do it again. However, if you will not be firm with the actions, it will know that following instructions is not really important and you are not the authority that they need to follow.

- They Like Other Pets

This breed is really friendly with other pets and cat. Wegie does not care if you have other cat or pet inside the house. It loves the company and will not get too aggressive too them – this will not cause any issue with other pets. They will not confront this, including pets, kids, and even strangers. However, you might need to supervise the breed in the introduction of the pets.

- They Love Love!

Norwegian Forest Cats love to love their humans. This breed loves to spend quality time with their humans and other pets. You can sleep next it, cuddle, spend time with the

Chapter Two: Why Norwegian Forest Cat is Perfect for You

kids, and be close to you. They will not run away from you if you want to get love and attention.

- They Are Low Maintenance

Just give it a litter box, water, and food and your dog will do just fine. You can go out for a weekend and you do not need a pet sitter.

- They Are Entertaining

It is very entertaining to watch your cat go about and play around in different positions. They love to play wherever they can.

What's Bad About Them?

- Some might have hereditary issue

Some cat might carry a certain hereditary issue. Think that all Norwegian Forest Cat are generally healthy, however, if you bought your pet from a sketchy breeder, it may carry certain disease.

Chapter Two: Why Norwegian Forest Cat is Perfect for You

- It loves to scratch... anything

Having a cat means dealing with different furniture being scratched! You need to provide a separate scratching post to make sure that your furniture will not be ruined.

Traveling Overseas

If you plan to travel with your pet, you may need to do certain things before you even go to the airport. This holds true especially if you do not want to leave your precious pet with family or friends. Taking your pet to another place is time-consuming and complicated process, you should do extensive research before you go through the process. If you want to travel overseas, think of answers for the following questions?

- How long will I be gone?

If you are only traveling for a short period of time, it is advisable to give or entrust your pet to your family or friends, however, if you will be gone for a year or more, it is better to bring it with you.

Chapter Two: Why Norwegian Forest Cat is Perfect for You

- Will my pet be all right to travel in the airplane cargo?

Think if your pet will be all right to be in a confined place for a long period of time. Could it survive long hours?

- Would the quarantine affect my pet greatly?

Will the well-being of my cat be affected? It is worth the risk? These are just some questions that you need to answer.

Here are some things that you need to remember before you transport your pet elsewhere:

- Before You Go Out Of The Country

  - The concern of many countries with pets from overseas is the transmission of certain diseases. They are afraid that avian influenza and rabies might spread from birds to humans.

  - Rabies is the main concern for ferrets, dogs, and cats; you need to present a rabies vaccination to make sure that your cat does not have rabies.

  - Aside from this, you need to research how long the quarantine is for the country that you will be staying. Remember that you will not be with your pet during this quarantine period. A problem for this is the expensiveness of the quarantine, which could last up to six months!

- Other than this, there are strict import requirements for pet imports for specific countries.

- You also need to think about the possible health threats for your pets when it travels overseas. There is no specific immunization against the Avain flu or other dangerous disease or parasites that may affect your pet. Think, is it worth the risk?

- In-Transit With Your Pet

  - Some airlines may allow pets to travel in the cabin, only if you have a small cage that will fit under your seat.

  - Some airlines will restrict the pet transportation during certain times of the year. Research on the air pressure and temperature in the cargo before you book the flight.
  - It is better for your pet if your flight is direct and has a short travel time.

Chapter Two: Why Norwegian Forest Cat is Perfect for You

- Research on the specific requirements for the airlines when it comes to transportation of the pet inside the cabin.

- Before the travel, make sure you have trained your cat to be inside the crate or kennel. You can add toys and pieces of clothing so your pet will be very familiar during the transportation.
- Find pet-friendly airlines before you book a flight.

- Money Matters

  - If you travel with your pet overseas, it is a very expensive affair.

  - Make sure you list down all the costs you need before you book your flight.

  - You may need to pay for the vaccinations and health certificates before the flight, which could be very costly.

  - The cost of traveling with your pet is steadily increasing overtime.

Chapter Two: Why Norwegian Forest Cat is Perfect for You

- ◦ If you do not want your pet to travel with you in a cabin, you may need to travel it through the cargo.

- ◦ You need to remember that shipping your pet in a pressurized cargo of the airplane.

- The Way Back Home

  - ◦ Taking your pet home is another issue.

  - ◦ Your country may need to be quarantined again if you decide to go home.

These are just some things that you need to remember if you want to travel with your pet. You need to weigh the pros and cons before you decide to book a flight. If this is the first time to travel, you may want to keep your pet in your home country with a close relative.

What Does My Norwegian Forest Cat Need?

Having a new pet at home is very exciting! You will have a cute playful, cuddly, little furball in your arms. Your

Chapter Two: Why Norwegian Forest Cat is Perfect for You

pet will grow into a wonderful adult cat that could be your best friend in the future.

You can start of the great relationship with your pet through getting things ready before it arrives. You may need to spend money to getting things right.

KITTY LITTER... AND A LOT OF PATIENCE

A kitty litter is important to have in your house. This litter will be used every day by your cat, mainly because the cat is trained to poop or pee in the same area each time. You will not need to scoop poop in the backyard, but you will really need to buy a kitty litter for it.

You can buy a simple plastic tray or an innovative poop handler. The concept heavily depends on your preference and budget. However, you may need to notice the characteristics of your cat, if your cat is not comfortable in using the box, a reason is that it does not like the litter. You need to experiment and try another brand, until your cat is fully satisfied and comfortable in using it.

A COMFORTABLE AND LUXURIOUS BED

Any pet would want to have the place to call its own, and a bed is a special way for your pet to have its own area.

Chapter Two: Why Norwegian Forest Cat is Perfect for You

You will have lot of choices if you ever shop bed for your cat. You can buy a simple pillow or a nesty - type of bed. However, cats might want to sleep elsewhere, like on the couch or even the bed with you. But, you can still buy the kitty bed for your Norwegian Forest Cat.

A STURDY SCRATCHING POST

Norwegian Forest Cat, just like other cats, really love to scratch! They need and they will scratch wherever it will be! However, you might need to consider getting a scratching post to have a designated post that is made for scratching.

There are a lot of choices for the post the you will be buying, there are a lot of varieties and brands that you will encounter. In this part, we will be giving you tips to find the best scratching post for your pet:

- **STABLE AND STURDY**
    - You need to choose the scratching post that your cat can hit very hard and play vigorously. The post must remain upright and in place.

- **TALL**
    - You should have a 25-30 inches tall scratching post.

Chapter Two: Why Norwegian Forest Cat is Perfect for You

- ○ The post must be high so your cat can have a lot of area to scratch.

- **VERTICAL**
  - ○ Your cat post should be vertical, because cats like that, however, if your pet does not like it vertically, you may need to store it in a horizontal position.

WATER AND FOOD BOWLS

You need to find a sturdy water and food bowls for your cat. You may need to buy the stainless steel bowl because it is very easy to sterilize and clean. You can also buy ceramic or glass bowls, plastics are not recommended because it will host bacteria that could potentially kill your pet. Make sure that the bowls are shallow, so your cat could be comfortable to eat or drink from it.

A LOT OF TOYS

Kittens love to play, and playtime is a crucial component in their physical and emotional development. Cat toys are essential during their playtime and any toys could be vital to your cat's development. However, you need to make sure that any small pieces will not fall off the toy. Do not give a toy that is smaller than a ping - pong ball, because it is a choking hazard.

GROOMING TOOLS

Grooming tools are important for your cat to look good and feel good. Keep your tools at a minimum because Norwegian Forest Cats hardly sheds and can cope up with different seasons easily.

You may want to buy basic brushes and comb for weekly brushing. Aside from this, a good grooming scissors are needed for this task. You should not use your kitchen scissors as these are not really effective in cutting the fur.

CARRIER AND COLLAR

You may want to put a collar to your cat. Collars are important to keep track where your cat is. Make sure that the collar will not break away or snap away easily. However, having collars to your cat is a big task; you need to train your cat on how to use this every day. Other than this, you may want to buy a cat carrier. The carrier is the safest way for you to transport your cat either to the vets or just some random driving. You may want to train your cat to stay and behave in the carrier.

Chapter Two: Why Norwegian Forest Cat is Perfect for You
CAT FOOD AND TREATS

Cat food and treats are very essential to the overall health of your Norwegian Forest Cat. In the cat food, you should search about the nutritional values that your cat can get from there, make sure that you thoroughly read the label to know about the food that your cat will eat. Cat treats, as yummy as they may sound, are only given once in a while. You can use these treats as rewards for them, either in exhibiting great behaviour, following commands, or during your training session – you heard it right! You can train cats! Read on to know more about training your cat!

The aforementioned things are the needed things before your Norwegian Forest Cat goes home. They may be a lot of thing, but it is better to be prepared rather than to frantically run to the store and finds the things that you need. In this chapter, we have carefully summarized the positive and negative traits of our beloved Norwegian Forest Cat – have you decided yet? Are you willing to take the risk and enjoy this ride with your cat? If yes, let us move on! If no, read on to know more about the fantastic world of the Norwegian Forest Cat.

Chapter Three: Finding the Norwegian Forest Cat Suited For You

There are many choices as to what kind of pet you would want to have. You can buy a kitten or an adult cat for your home. The choice heavily relies on your preference. There are many things you need to consider before making up your mind, luckily, we are here to help. In this chapter, we will be giving you guidelines as to what kind of Norwegian Forest Cat you might want to buy.

In the world of the Norwegian Forest Cat, both cats and kittens are good choices; however, we will discuss further their advantages and disadvantages. The choice is

Chapter Three: Finding the Norwegian Forest Cat Suited For You

totally up to you! Read this chapter and know the tell - tale signs of the suited cat for you... have fun in your journey!

Kitten or Adult: What Shall I Choose?

You have already made up your mind in buying your Norwegian Forest Cat. However, there are things that you still need to decide before you have a happy home: What kind of cat should I choose? Some people prefer buying kittens, while some settle for adult cats. Whatever your choice may be, you still need to take care of them fully. Both adults and kitties have their own pros and cons, they have their own needs and wants however, you still need to choose wisely.

In this section, we will be help you decide what kind of cat you need to choose. Open your eyes and heart to the following choices:

Kittens

Kittens are clumsy, tiny, yet fluffy that will make anyone say 'awww'. It can be compared to a little, hyper child. This kitten is a great addition to your home if you want softness and love that will accompany you for years. They truly loved to be cuddled and loved whenever they can

Chapter Three: Finding the Norwegian Forest Cat Suited For You

get it. However, there are many things you need to do when you buy a kitten.

Here are some advantages if you ever want to take care of a kitten:

- Kittens are easier to train and socialize, whether you will train it to use litter box or having a cuddle session.

- Kittens are less prone to trouble. They will not get tangled in cods, fall from high places, or eat foreign things.

- Kittens are easier to introduce to new people, cats, or even pets.

- Having kittens can also be beneficial to your health and emotional well-being. It can lower your blood pressure and cholesterol.

- Getting kittens could teach you and your little children about daily responsibility, because there are a lot of things you need to take care of kittens.

- Kittens can help you in your social life. It can establish connections with other pet owners within

Chapter Three: Finding the Norwegian Forest Cat Suited For You

your area. You can meet new people during your weekly visits to the supermarket or drug store.

- If there are advantages, there are disadvantages of getting a kitten, these are:

- If you get a very young kitten, you may need to bottle feed it.

- You need to get all the vaccines and booster shots throughout its first year in the world.

- Kittens will stay with you for a very long time, especially if you will maintain its overall health.

- You may need to wait for the kitten season to get one

Adult Cats

An adult cat is also another option for you if you want to purchase a cat. An adult cat has its own advantages and disadvantage. Some people prefer this because they are already house trained, while some do not want this because some have attitude problems. If you are still hesitating to buy an adult cat, here are the advantages:

Chapter Three: Finding the Norwegian Forest Cat Suited For You

- What you see is what you get. An adult cat has fully developed, so you can see the exact the body type, eye color, and coat. Your cat could be laid back or active, vocal or quiet, demanding or cuddly because your cat has already developed itself.
- An adult cat can still bond with you just like a kitten. Your adult cat could even give more affection because it appreciates you for taking them in.

Here are some disadvantages of getting a cat:
- You may be getting a cat with a behavioural issue; however, you could still retrain it to fix its behaviour.

A Rescued Cat for Your Big Heart

You can also get a rescued cat. A rescue cat would shower you with great love and affection should you decide to take it home. A word of caution, you may need to retrain your cat to make it fully comfortable and settled in your home.

There are several rescue website that will offer you help in finding your preferred Norwegian Forest Cat. Remember, these rescued cats will love you dearly for taking it home and giving it its own shelter. You should visit the rescue site to fully inspect the cat, other than this, you need

Chapter Three: Finding the Norwegian Forest Cat Suited For You

to see how the cat socializes as it may have problems that you do not easily spot when the cat is alone.

A Reputable Norwegian Forest Cat Breeder

Finding a reputable cat breeder is a difficult task. You need to find and join a cat community to know where and who to buy your pet from. You do not easily trust the first breeder that you see, especially those in the online community. You can ask for help from your friends and family, especially if they are in the cat breeding or even in the pet breeding era.

Many people would tell you not to buy from a pet store, but this choice is entirely up to you. People who buy from pet stores are those who do not have enough time to scour different places and get to know everyone.

Find cat breeders that would want the best for their kittens/cat. Find people who would ask you questions and, aside from that, give it the best care possible through giving it medical needs; finding a cat from a reputable and lengthy task, but you need to find the best one possible for your pet and your future.

Chapter Three: Finding the Norwegian Forest Cat Suited For You

You can also find reputable breeders in cat shows, you can also see the different breeds in action, and decide whether the Norwegian Forest Cat is truly right for you. In shows, you can talk to breeders and enthusiasts and get all the information you would want.

Here are the things to look out for a reputable cat breeder:

What Should I Look For in A Reputable Cat Breeder?

There are signs or guidelines that you can consider if you want to find a reputable Norwegian Forest Cat breeder:

- Reputable breeders will not sell to pet stores because they would want to find the best home for their cats. Breeders would find the best homes for their kittens, they would ask you questions about yourself to make sure that you are a great fit for the kitten.

- Breeders will not sell you kittens less than ten weeks of age. Responsible breeders will first take care of the cats and give it its initial vaccinations and boosters. They would also do initial vet consultations to know if the kittens are sick or healthy.

Chapter Three: Finding the Norwegian Forest Cat Suited For You

- They might even suggest you spay or neuter your cat. They would ask things like what's your purpose in buying a Norwegian Forest Cat, if you will not use them for breeding, your breeder would suggest this one. However, the final decision will always be yours.
- The breeder would always guarantee you great cat health and replacement. They would let you sign a contract that would guarantee you can return the cat if ever you change the mind.

- In the said contract, the breeder will write down the terms of sale. This is to protect you and the breeder.

You need to remember that your Norwegian Forest Cat could live up to 20 years, so you need to find a healthy and happy cat that you can take care of. Do not buy impulsively; do not choose a cat or a kitten because 'it looks pretty'. Backyard, experienced breeders might sell more, but you can be slightly assured that the cat would be of great health.

Chapter Three: Finding the Norwegian Forest Cat Suited For You

A Healthy and Happy Norwegian Forest Cat

When you have decided where you will buy the cat, it is now the time to know whether the cat you are buying is healthy and happy. Make sure that you go through each of these things before you choose the cat from the litter:

- It should have clear and bright eyes.
- It should not have any form of discharge, whether clear or colored.
- The ears must be free from any discharge and clean. It should not be red or have a foul odor.
- The cat's gum should be pink, teeth free from any plaque or tartar. The breath must smell good.
- The coat should be clean and shiny.
- A healthy cat is not overweight.

WHAT IS NOT NORMAL FOR CATS?

- The cat should not have a diarrhea. Make sure that the poo is not too bloody or wet.
- See if there is blood or even traces of blood in the urine. Blood in urine indicates a problem for the cat.

Chapter Three: Finding the Norwegian Forest Cat Suited For You

These are just some of the characteristics of a happy and healthy Norwegian Forest Cat breed. Make sure to note of these things as you need to notice these characteristics from the breed. We have summarized to you what kind of cat you can get and where you can get it. Let us continue our journey in knowing a Norwegian Forest Cat.

Chapter Four: Taking Your Norwegian Forest Cat Home

Cats are amazing creature. They are aloof little creatures who still love being loved by their humans. The Norwegian Forest Cat is notoriously known to be quite loving and affectionate; they would stay with their human's side for long periods of time, however, they are selective to whom they will give their trust to and they are not afraid to say no.

In this chapter, we will be welcoming your Norwegian Forest Cat in your home. These steps are important because you and your pet are transitioning into a new phase in your life. You may be quite afraid at first, but you will go along with your pet soon enough.

Chapter Four: Taking Your Norwegian Forest Cat Home

Let us enjoy the ride and learn more about our beloved pet.

Living Spaces for Our Norwegian Forest Cat

Giving a suitable living space for your cat is essential to your cat's overall health and well-being.

You should give it a comfortable house with enough space that is enough for your pet's mental and physical stimulation, pet interaction, and human socialization.

If you only brought home one cat, it may require more contact and place to play. You may need to provide several activities to stimulate its brain and keep it company. However, if you have multiple cats, it will become comfortable easily and will become less stressed.

Your house should be suitable to the needs of however many cats you would want to have. It should be clean and well-maintained to provide a happy and healthy environment for it. You may even need to provide the cat with its own quiet space when it needs to be, this could be its 'bedroom' where it could sleep wherever it can.

You should also put the litter box in a private area. Your cat does not want to be 'exposed' whenever it needs to go pee or poo. Other than this, your cat should be able to run and walk freely at any time it may want.

Chapter Four: Taking Your Norwegian Forest Cat Home

Here is a simple checklist that you need to accomplish before bringing your Norwegian Forest Cat at home:

- Private quiet space
- A place for the scratching post
- A space for a quiet, private, and clean litter box
- An outdoor area
- Enough floor space for activity, resting, sleeping, defecation, and etc.
- Item and toys that would stimulate brain function.
- Separate spaces to eat and drink.

Aside from this knowledge, you should also provide the following things for your cat:

CAT BED AND BEDDING

If you ever plan to make your pet sleep on your bed or any other surface, it is till best to give it its own place to space. You can bring home a cat bed and add soft blankets or towels. Make sure that these things are made of washable materials because you need to wash and clean them every week.

Chapter Four: Taking Your Norwegian Forest Cat Home

Ensure that the bed is in a nice quiet area – this will serve as its 'own spot' inside the house.

CARRIERS

You can transport your Norwegian Forest Cat easily through a cat carrier. Many carriers can feet under airplane seats, so your cat can travel with you anywhere you would want. This carrier is also useful to transport your cat when going to the vet. Put a blanket inside the carrier to provide comfort and warmth. You can also add any toys to provide entertainment for your cat.

It is not advisable to buy wicker baskets as your cat will scratch it endlessly, and will just end up being ruined. Aside from this, you also need to buy a slightly bigger carrier so your cat can be comfortable inside the carrier.

LITTER AND ITS LITTER BOX

Provide a clean and private litter box for your cat can add to the comfortability of our beloved furry friend, the Norwegian Forest Cat. Cats are known to be naturally clean and have a strict waste process. They want to have a clean and private environment to poo and pee.

Chapter Four: Taking Your Norwegian Forest Cat Home

You need to put the litter box away from any other spaces from which your cat eats, plays, sleeps. You can put it in a utility room or even the corner of your bathroom. Further, the box itself must be wide for your cat's entry and exit (the size does not really matter, you could buy cardboard, plastic, or metal – it is just up to your preference). You can choose a bigger box for your cat, your Wegie should have enough place to kick litter to their soiled space. Your cat is pretty certain with their locations, so you need to make sure that once you have placed the litter box – you will not move it anymore.

According to research, cats prefer clumping clay litter. This litter will turn urine and feces into clumps that could easily be scooped out and remove. They also like unscented litter. If you ever plan to buy your own litter, make sure it is not small enough to be ingested by your kitten, it could lead to gastrointestinal discomfort.

You should have one litter box per floor of the house plus another one. If you have multiple cats, each will need its own litter box. As a rule, you need to clean and scoop out your litter box at least once each day. By the end of the week, make sure you throw all the litter away and clean the litter box with water and soap then pour a new layer of litter.

Chapter Four: Taking Your Norwegian Forest Cat Home
SCRATCHING POST

Your cat loves and needs to scratch. This habit makes them fully stretch out their bodies and to eliminate dead sheaths in their nails. If you do not want your household items to be the post, you need to purchase a scratching post. The length must be at least three feet, and should be covered with sisal or carpet.

The post must be sturdy so your post will not fall when bumped by your cat. You need to place the post in the play area so it can be easily noticed by your cat. You can spice up their play time by putting the post horizontally or vertically.

Aside from knowing what should be in the house, you should also know what should not be in your house. In this next section, we will talk about how to cat-proof your home.

CAT PROOFING 101

Cat Proofing Tip #1: Keep the food off your counters especially when you are not around, keep it somewhere your cat could not access.

Cat Proofing Tip #2: Stow away all the cords by tying them up or putting them up behind the top of the blinds. If you

Chapter Four: Taking Your Norwegian Forest Cat Home

think that your cat would play with the blinds, you better change your blinds immediately.

Cat Proofing Tip #3: You may also keep your plants away from your cats. You do not know what plants are poisonous to them. Your cat may accidentally eat it or play with it.

Cat Proofing Tip #4: Your cat likes to stay in warm, dark spots where they would fit inside and snuggle. Check your washer and dryer before you use them, you might not know that your cat is happily napping inside of it. Aside from this, make sure that your cat would not go near the hot stove, so always make sure that they are not near it.

Cat Proofing Tip #5: Your cat love to play with the garland and Christmas ball. Make sure they are sturdy enough that your cat won't knock it off easily, or better yet, do not hang decorations that might entice them.

These are just some things that you need to remember when you bring your cat at home. You might encounter some more problems, so better research on them more.

Chapter Four: Taking Your Norwegian Forest Cat Home

Chapter Five: Feeding Your Norwegian Forest Cat Yummy and Nutritious Food

We are halfway through knowing our beloved Norwegian Forest Cat. We have learned its rich background, basic characteristics, where to buy it, and how to deal with its household set-up. Now, we will further our knowledge through knowing what it eats.

Nutrition is a key component in keeping your cat happy and healthy. You need to ensure that your cat will get all the needed nutrition for optimum growth and long life. You might be hesitant to make mistake, but it is okay to make mistakes and learn from it! In this chapter, we will give you an overview about the nutritional guide for the Norwegian Forest Cat.

Chapter Five: Feeding Your Norwegian Forest Cat Yummy and Nutritious Food

Wants vs. Needs: What's More Important?

You might be tempted to give your cat its treats most of the time. However, it might not be the best for your cat. You need to give it the necessary cat food that contains all the nutrients that your cat needs. Aside from this, do not give them too much table scraps as this is not really needed by them.

Your Norwegian Forest Cat's Nutritional Needs

Here are the basic nutritional needs by your cat:

PROTEIN

The protein gives amino acids that are needed to manufacture antibodies, hormones, enzymes, and tissues. This will provide your cat energy, and helps them for development and growth.

FAT

Fat helps the body to produce energy. This also aids in nutrient transportation and utilization. It is involved in metabolic regulation and cell integrity.

Chapter Five: Feeding Your Norwegian Forest Cat Yummy and Nutritious Food

MINERALS

Minerals are needed to almost all of the physiological activity of your Norwegian Forest Cat. This contributes greatly to pH balance, oxygen transportation, enzyme formation, and nutrient utilization.

VITAMINS

Vitamins are needed for normal growth and function and metabolism regulation. This is usually found in several foods, but some are found in the animal's body. Some needed vitamins are A, D, E, K, C, B complex.

WATER

Water is needed by your cat, especially if it likes to eat dry food and treats. Your cat can be dehydrated through eating kibble, because their body is not programmed to drink water.

These are just some of the things that you need to know about the nutritional needs of your Norwegian Forest Cat. In the following sections, we will be giving you tips and techniques in feeding your cat.

Chapter Five: Feeding Your Norwegian Forest Cat Yummy and Nutritious Food

Choosing the Right Food for Wegie

Here are some of the things you need to answer to know that if the cat food is really right for your cat:

Can The Cat Food Provide All The Nutrition My Cat Would Need?

Cat foods are often labeled as "complete", "balanced" or etc., however, you should be able to read labels to make sure that your cat will be getting enough nutrients, not just like because the packaging says "complete".

Is The Cat Food "Complete and Balanced"? Is This Always the Right Choice?

Some people do not believe that the cat food is enough to feed their cat. They opt to have additional supplements, treats, and vitamins that would suffice other needs. Open your hearts to this option.

Which Food Is the Best For My Norwegian Forest Cat?

There are a lot of food choices for your cat; you might have a hard time in choosing what the best is for it. However, you

Chapter Five: Feeding Your Norwegian Forest Cat Yummy and Nutritious Food

must learn to identify what kind of food your cat would eat in the wild. It should be minimally processed, have moisture, contains enough nutrition. The choice is up to you, your budget and lifestyle.

The Main Food Choices for Your Cat

There are many cat food choices for your pet. You have a whole shelf that you must scrutinize one by one, however, the basic ingredient the cat food must have is meat. In this section, we will help you decide what kind of cat food you can give to your cat:

COMMERCIALLY MADE vs. HOMEMADE

Homemade food is an option by pet owners to make sure that the cat will have adequate water and you will have full control over all of the things you will put there. On the other hand, if you are a very busy person, the conventional commercial premium food is often convenient and often cheaper. The choice heavily relies on your preference.

The raw meat is more nutritional, but it takes hard work. However, people recommend to give both a mixture of home cooked meal and commercial.

Chapter Five: Feeding Your Norwegian Forest Cat Yummy and Nutritious Food

RAW MEAT vs. COOKED MEAT

If you give raw meat, the meat might contain parasites that will be harmful to your pet's body; on the other hand, cooked meat will lose some of its nutrients because of the processing. As a cat owner, you could give a combination of the two.

Kinds of Commercial Cat Food

There are three main types of cat food. The main difference lies on the processing method and water content.

- **DRY FOOD** – only contain 10% moisture and 90% matter. The food includes kibbles, biscuits, cereals that are fitted for the cat. This contains high number of protein, which could suffice its need. However, you may still need to give water or gravy to suffice its water requirement.

- **SEMI-MOIST FOOD** – This contains 25-45% of moisture and 55-75% matter. It is made of chewy moist pellet and is sold in sachets. This option is more

Chapter Five: Feeding Your Norwegian Forest Cat Yummy and Nutritious Food

expensive than dry food and actually quite smaller, however, it has high palatability and used as cat treats.

- **WET FOOD** – Contains 90% moisture and 10% matter. Made into cans, trays, pouches that will contain different forms of chunks in jelly or gravy. These are the most expensive among the choices, but usually the yummiest.

As a cat owner, you should give a variety of these three choices. Give these three things to your cat and see what it likes best. Each food has its own advantages and disadvantages.

Feeding Amount and Frequency

Feeding your cat is not that easy, there are a lot of options and only a few people to ask questions too. If you feed your cat too little or give the cat the wrong food, your cat will get sick. If you give it too much, it will get fat. In this section, we will help you know how much you need to give and how often you need to feed your cat. You need to answer these questions to know more about your cat:

Chapter Five: Feeding Your Norwegian Forest Cat Yummy and Nutritious Food

HOW OLD IS MY CAT?

Age is a crucial factor to knowing how much to give your cat. Kittens need more food per pound of their body weight, this is used to support their weight, so you need to feed your cat more throughout the day. Some says that kittens need to eat up to three times a day from birth to three month. From six months to adulthood, you should feed your cat two times a day. When it reaches one year, you should only feed your cat once or twice daily.

HOW HEALTHY IS YOUR CAT?

If you see your cat becoming sick or ill, you should contact your vet immediately. It is best to treat the disease then feed your cat normally. When your cat ages, its teeth may go bad, so you can feed it with canned food.

What Not To Give To Your Cat

If there *are foods* that you can give your cat, there are still *foods* that are poisonous to your cat. The food mentioned should not be given to your cat at any case possible:

Chapter Five: Feeding Your Norwegian Forest Cat Yummy and Nutritious Food

- Alcohol
- Chocolate
- Coffee
- Tea
- Energy Drinks
- Dairy
- Fat Trimmings
- Raw Meat
- Raw Eggs
- Raw Fish
- Grapes
- Raisins
- Onions
- Garlic
- Xylitol

If your cat has accidentally ingested one of these things, contact your vet immediately. These things are just some of the important reminders that you need to know about feeding your cat. Make sure you follow these things so your cat can be happy and healthy.

Chapter Five: Feeding Your Norwegian Forest Cat Yummy and Nutritious Food

Chapter Six: Time to Groom Your Norwegian Forest Cat

Grooming is a task that you need to do every week or every two weeks. If you are a busy person, you can bring your cat to the groomer and let it do his/her job. However, you still need to know these things because you do not know when an emergency will occur.

In this chapter, we will be teaching you the basics of cat grooming. This will include brushing, bathing, nail clipping, and etc. Aside from this, we will give you a list of the needed tool for this task.

Chapter Six: Time to Groom Your Norwegian Forest Cat

Make the Grooming Task Enjoyable

The grooming session needs to be fun for both you and your cat. Make sure that your cat is relaxed when you groom it, you could do it after exercise or after eating. You need to train your cat to remember the task as a positive one, so you do not need to lose your temper. If you are stressed out or in a bad mood, you should not groom your cat.

Make your grooming time for about five to 10 minutes. Lengthen the routine until your pet is get used to this routine. You should also train your pet to be handled and cuddled. Pet your cat in every area, such as its back, feed, tail, ears, and belly.

You need to extend your patience during this process. Remember to praise and give treats to your cat when the grooming session is over.

BRUSHING YOUR CAT'S FUR

A regular brushing session is needed to keep your cat's fur in good condition. This task will remove dirt, distribute natural oils throughout its coat, remove and prevent tangles, and keep the skin clear of anything. Here are just some things you need to do when brushing your cat's fur:

Chapter Six: Time to Groom Your Norwegian Forest Cat

- Use a metal comb and comb the fur from head to tail.

- Use a rubber brush and bristle to remove loose or dead hair.

- Be gentle in brushing the belly and chest area.

- If there is fur in the tail area, part it down the middle and brush the fur to either side.

BATHING YOUR CAT

If your cat's fur becomes oily and greasy, or if she has put something sticky or smelly in its body, it is time for a bath. You need to use a mild shampoo that is safe for your cat. Here are some steps to bathing your cat:

- Brush the cat's fur to remove all the mats and dead hair.

- Put the rubber mat in the tub or sink to avoid slipping.

- Place three to four inches of water in the tub, then put your cat in it.

- Use spray hose to wet your cat, do not spray directly to the nose, ears, or eyes. If you do not use a hose, use a large plastic pitcher.

Chapter Six: Time to Groom Your Norwegian Forest Cat

- Massage the shampoo in the body, work from head up to the tail.

- Rinse your cat thoroughly and avoid the nose, ears, and eyes.

- Dry your pet using a towel.

CLIPPING YOUR CAT'S NAIL

Handling your cat only when clipping its nail is a terrible idea, this is because your cat will get anxious and stress out if you do this task. What you need to do is get your cat used to having its cat touch before you clip the nails. Rub your hand on their nail and gently press the toes while giving treats and praise. Here is how you trim your cat's nails:

- Apply a gentle pressure on the top of the food and the cushiony pad to make your cat release its claws.

- Use high quality sharp cat nail scissors to cut only the white tip of the nail, just before the nail starts to curl.

- Avoid the vein that runs through the nail, this is seen as the pink area.

Chapter Six: Time to Groom Your Norwegian Forest Cat

- If you accidentally cut the vein, it may bleed, so you need to apply some styptic powder to it.

Tools of the Trade

Here are the five essential grooming tools that you need to own when grooming your cat. Make sure you have these things before you start your grooming session:

NAIL CLIPPERS

This is usually inexpensive, easy to use, and the quickest way to assure that your cat will not ruin anything when it is scratching something. There are a lot of nail clippers available, it is totally up to your preference to choose the best kind. Cat claw scissors are available for you.

BRUSHES JUST FOR YOUR CAT

There are a lot of brushes available for your cat. These are specifically designed for certain cat types, while some are used for specific purpose. You need to use a bristle brush, fine tooth comb for this task.

Chapter Six: Time to Groom Your Norwegian Forest Cat

PET WIPES AND SPRAYS: A NEW WAY?

These wipes are moist disposable towels that can quickly touch up or used in a full bath. These are just some of the things that you need to purchase to fully groom your cat. These tools might be intimidating at first but you will learn from it through practice.

Chapter Seven: Tips for Showing Your Norwegian Forest Cat

Norwegian Forest Cat is a smart little furball. They can be trained to do whatever they want to be. One thing to train for is cat shows. This breed is truly agile and flexible, so you can truly show off this breed during different shows. In this chapter, we will be dealing with the breed standards as well as show tips and regulations. Take note of these things if ever you want to enter your Norwegian Forest Cat in shows.

Chapter Seven: Tips for Showing Your Norwegian Forest Cat

Point Scores in Shows

HEAD (60)
Nose Profile	10
Muzzle	10
Ears	10
Eye Shape	5
Eye Set	5
Neck	5
Chin	5

BODY (30)
Torso	10
Legs/Feet	5
Boning	5
Tail	5
COAT LENGTH/TEXTURE	10
COLOR/PATTERN	5
BALANCE	5

The Norwegian Forest Cat Breed Standard

Chapter Seven: Tips for Showing Your Norwegian Forest Cat

GENERAL
- It is a sturdy cat.
- It has a double coat.
- It is a slowly maturing breed. They are in full growth only at the fifth year of their life.

HEAD
- All sides of its head are of equal length.
- Its neck is heavily muscled and short.

NOSE PROFILE
- Its nose is straight from its brow ridge up to the tip.
- The flat forehead continues to a gentle curved neck and skull.

CHIN:
- Its chin is firm.
- It should be in line with the nose.
- It should be gently rounded.

MUZZLE:
- It should be straight that extends up to the base of the ear.
- It should be without whisker pad and no pinch.

Chapter Seven: Tips for Showing Your Norwegian Forest Cat

EARS:
- It should medium to large
- The tip must be rounded with a broad base.
- It should look alert with the cup of the ear pointing sideways.
- The pair must be heavily furnished.

EYES:
- Almond shaped
- large
- well opened
- expressive
- It should be at a slight angle with outer corner higher than its opposite corner.

BODY:
- Well-balanced
- solidly muscled
- moderate length
- substantial bone structure
- It shows powerful appearance through its broad chest with girth and no fat.
- It has a great depth of flank
- Males are imposing and large
- Females are smaller and more refined.

Chapter Seven: Tips for Showing Your Norwegian Forest Cat

LEGS:
- front legs are shorter than hind legs
- the rumps are higher than its shoulders
- heavily muscled thighs
- it should have large round, firm paws

TAIL:
- Long and bushy
- It should have a broader base
- it should have an equal length from the base of neck to base of tail
- It should have guard hairs
-

COAT:
- It should have a distinguishable double coat.
- It has a dense undercoat that is covered with smooth, glossy, long, water resistant guard hairs that falls on its side.
- It has three sections for its bib: short collar, side mutton chops, and frontal ruff.
- The coat may appear fuller during winter time

Chapter Seven: Tips for Showing Your Norwegian Forest Cat

PATTERNS:
- every color and pattern is allowable with the except those that shows hybrid that results in colors of chocolate, sable, lavender, lilac, cinnamon, fawn.

COLORS AND PATTERN:
- The pattern and color must be distinct and clear
- The pattern must be well-marked and even for classic, mackerel, spotted cats.

DISQUALIFYING FEATURE
- There is a severe break in the nose.
- It has a square muzzle
- It possesses a whisker pinch, long rectangular body.
- The cat has incorrect number of toes, crossed eyes, kinked tail.
- Wegies that have delicate bone structure
- Any evidence of hybridization

Preparing Your Cat for the Show

If your cat complies with the breed standard, you might as well enter it in a show. However, there are things to

Chapter Seven: Tips for Showing Your Norwegian Forest Cat

prepare before the show itself. Make sure you go through these things before you enter it in a show.

KNOWING THE SHOW SCHEDULE

Cat shows are scheduled months before the actual performance. You may need to go through the internet or make a few calls to know more. You need to read the schedule very well to know more. It may seem scary at first, but it will pay off soon enough. If you are confused, you should phone a friend to know more.

FILL OUT THE ENTRY FORM

You might think this is a no-brainer, but many people fail this phase. You need to thoroughly read and check everything before submitting your form. Any mistakes in form can cause you disqualification.

CLEAN YOUR CAT

This is another no-brainer, but you must de-flea and de-worm your cat beforehand. Make sure there are no

Chapter Seven: Tips for Showing Your Norwegian Forest Cat

bruises, scars, or anything that could disqualify your cat. These are just some of the things that you need to know before showing your cat. It is a tedious process, but you will learn greatly from these tips.

Chapter Nine: Keeping Your Norwegian Foreign Cats Healthy and Safe

Chapter Eight: Building Your Relationship with Your Cat through Training

Catching, fetching, or stealing things are not really the forte of your beloved Norwegian Forest Cat. However, you can still train your cat to do other things, which could make it an amazing member of your household. Norwegian Forest Cats are naturally smart, they like to play and follow your commands, and so this task will be easy for you. But, you still need to be patient and persistent in training your cat. It will be a difficult task, but it will yield great results.

Chapter Nine: Keeping Your Norwegian Foreign Cats Healthy and Safe

Basic Cat Training

There are a lot of things that your cat needs to learn. These are basic things that will make your life and its life a breeze. Make sure you take time to teach these things or else your life will be miserable.

USING THE LITTER BOX

Using the litter box is not really a difficult task. Norwegian Forest Cats are usually clean and they have the tendency to bury their wastes. However, you still need to teach your cat on how to properly use its litter box:

- Put your cat and its clean litter box in a confined, secret area, like a specific room in your house.

- Make sure that your cat will have access to food and clean water.

- If your cat poops or pees outside of its litter box, you need to transfer the waste in the litter box. (this step is needed so that your cat will be attracted to the smell of the waste, and your cat will start using the box)

- When your cat is used to being in the litter box for a day or two, it will begin to use the box regularly.

Chapter Nine: Keeping Your Norwegian Foreign Cats Healthy and Safe

If your cat hasn't used the box after a couple of days, you need to change your way. After it has eaten, put the cat in the litter box, then 'scratch' the surface of the litter with the fingertip.

If the cat has not used it, you need to make sure that the box is clean. If it was used before, clean the box with baking soda and fill it with clean, new litter. You can also change the litter; some cats want a specific brand to be its nest. However, if your cat still does not want to use it, you need to consult your vet. There might be a problem that causes your cat to not use the box.

TEACHING GOOD BEHAVIOR

If your cat has done something wrong, and you do not want to repeat it, you need to train your cat not to do the behavior anymore. The first step in getting rid of the bad behavior knows why the cat is acting that way. The cat might believe that the behavior it has exhibited is perfectly all right.

If it claws your beloved furniture, it just means that your cat wants to claw something! Remember that your cat needs and wants to claw something – it is a part of their nature! To stop this behaviour, make sure you have a designated scratching post for the cat. However, if it still claws with the scratching post around, you need to train the cat stop this nasty behaviour. BUT, remember to train it using positive reinforcement, do not use punishment in any way. Do not hit your cat, it will not understand the reason why you behaved that way, and will just fear you.

TRAIN NOT TO BE AGGRESSIVE

Sometimes, your cat will play too rough, bite too much, or even scratch everything! This is another behavior that you can stop, at a certain degree. If you are in play session and your cat begins scratching or biting, scare your cat using a loud noise. You can clap your hands or make a hissing sound, just make any loud sound that will make your cat to stop the behaviour. After this, they will just walk away.

Do this act every time your cat gets too difficult, then, it will learn to stop biting and scratching especially during play time.

CAN YOU REALLY NOT TRAIN YOUR CAT?

Chapter Nine: Keeping Your Norwegian Foreign Cats Healthy and Safe

People often think that cats can't be trained; however, it is not really true. You should and you can train your cat to be an active and pleasant member of the family. You can, also, train them to do dog like tasks, such as sitting, or walking – however, this will come with a big price.

Five Things to Remember When I Train My Wegie

I SHOULD NOT PUNISH

Cats do not actually learn from 'discipline'. Aside from this, punishing your cat will just cause stress that will further lead to health and behavioral problems. You need to have positive reinforcement and patience especially when training your cat.

CLICKER AND TREATS ARE MY TOOLS

The clicker and treats are the two most important tools when training your cat. Clicker will give you positive reinforcement when training your cat.

During training sessions, you need to give your cat a treat if it follows a click; this is to signal that this is a desired

Chapter Nine: Keeping Your Norwegian Foreign Cats Healthy and Safe

behavior. Without the clicker or treats, your cat will be confused with your behavior.

TEACHING YOUR CAT TO COME

Your cat can respond to your cue and run away. You need to train a cat to follow you especially before feeding; you can make a distinct noise, before you open the can. Your pet will associate this sound to something positive, like giving food. Soon enough, your cat will go whenever you make the noise.

You can also use the clicker to further the training process. You can make the noise, use the clicker, and reward your cat when it comes. You can start the training in short distances, when the cat gets comfortable, you can continue it to longer distances. The training session should be two times a day, with five minutes or less. Within the span of this time, you should have repeated the behavior up to twenty times.

BE PLEASANT, SHAKE HANDS!

Your cat could certainly shake hands too! Just ready

Chapter Nine: Keeping Your Norwegian Foreign Cats Healthy and Safe

the treat and level yourself with the cat. Pat the cat's paw while you say the word 'shake. You can use your trusty old clicker to move the paw.

You need to repeat the task until the cat offer its paw when you say the word shake without the tapping. This could take a few training sessions over a couple of days.

IS IT OKAY TO BEG?

Training your cat to beg is another trick that you can teach your cat. This trick is just the same with 'shaking hands'.

In this care, hold the treat above the head and give the command to beg. Your cat needs to stand on its hind legs and reach up for the treat, make the clicking sound to show that the behavior is acknowledge – then give the treat. You need to practice this until your cat is okay without the treat above its head.

WALKING ON A LEASH: ONLY A DOG'S TASK?

You need to buy a harness that will attach on its back, not the neck. You need to put the harness before you leave

Chapter Nine: Keeping Your Norwegian Foreign Cats Healthy and Safe

for a couple of days wherever it goes, just like its feeding area or its favorite spot to sleep. This will make your cat accustomed to the behavior

You, then, need to drape over the harness then give the treat. After your cat is okay with this, you need to secure the harness and leave it on your cat for a couple of minutes, then move it up to a couple of days.

Once your cat is okay with being in a harness, you need to attach the leash and let your cat wander around the house freely.

After your cat is okay with the task, you need to hold the leash during your training session. Slowly, get them to be okay with it in the outdoors. You need to take your cat in a new area, but you need to start with somewhere quiet.

These are just some of the things you need to remember when training your cat. It might sound difficult or too tiring, but this is a very rewarding task. Training your cat to do new things will enable it to become a productive member of your family. Make sure you spend time to actually train it, and also persist on training it every day.

Chapter Nine: Keeping Your Norwegian Foreign Cats Healthy and Safe

Chapter Nine: Keeping Your Norwegian Forest Cat Healthy and Safe

You just do not purchase a cat because you want it during its happy days. Having a cat with you entails that you will be with it during its sad days also. And most of the times, the sad days are the hardest for you and your cat. Taking care of your cat during its sick days is difficult and somehow overwhelming. But, you can prevent some diseases through health check-ups and vaccinations.

In this section, we will give you an insight on the vaccination schedule and other related things that will keep your Norwegian Forest Cat healthy and happy. This is important so better have your lucky pen ready and starts the task easily.

Why Should I Vaccine My Norwegian Forest Cat?

As costly as it may sound, you need to vaccine your cat especially when you got it in a very young stage. Remember, the mother may have given antibodies to prevent common diseases, but these are not enough. Your

Chapter Nine: Keeping Your Norwegian Foreign Cats Healthy and Safe

cat needs additional protection against common ailments. Here is the vaccination schedule for our beloved kittens and cats:

Six to Eight Weeks of Age

- Core vaccines are needed, especially for feline distemper, feline calicivirus, feline rhinotracheitis
- You also need to ask your vet if you need to have a vaccine against chlamydia

The core vaccines must be given every three to four weeks, the final kitten vaccinations should be given at 14 to 16 weeks of age.

Ten to Twelve Weeks of Age

- Second vaccination of the core vaccines
- You may also ask your vet about the feline leukaemia

12 – 16 Weeks of Age

- Your vet should administer the rabies shot

14-16 Weeks of Age

- Third round of vaccination for the core vaccines

Chapter Nine: Keeping Your Norwegian Foreign Cats Healthy and Safe

1 Year of Age

- Vaccination of core vaccines
- Rabies
- You can also add the chlamydia and feline leukaemia.

Getting a Thorough Cat Check-Up

Cats, just like other animals, easily hide their medical conditions, until it is too advanced to be fixed by anyone. This is a good sign for you to have your cat thoroughly examined at least once a year, for young to teenagers, and twice a year for senior dogs.

THOROUGH PHYSICAL EXAMINATION

Here are the components of a thorough and complete physical examination for your cat. You need to know these things as not to get shocked with what the vet would do to your cat:

Chapter Nine: Keeping Your Norwegian Foreign Cats Healthy and Safe

- Assessing its overall appearance and alertness: Is the cat alert, responsive, or bright?

- Looking at its gait: Is there a sign of lameness, stiffness, or asymmetry?

- Examining the hair and skin coat: Is there a sign of hair loss or a skin inflammation? Is the coat good that well conforms to the breed? Are there weird bumps on the cat's body?

- Grading the body condition score (bcs): Your cat will be assessed from 1-9, the number indicates if the cat is underweight, overweight, or just right. A 5 score indicates the ideal body weight, 1-4 indicates signs of being too thin, while 6-9 indicates that the cat is too heavy.

- Measuring the cat's:
    - Body weight in kilograms or pounds
    - Body temperature, the normal temperature should be 100-102 Fahrenheit

    - The normal respiratory rate is around 16-28 breaths per minute

Chapter Nine: Keeping Your Norwegian Foreign Cats Healthy and Safe

- o The number of seconds of the gum line to be pink should be 1-1.5 seconds

- Overall examination of the ears, nose, eyes, and oral activity: Are there signs of abnormalities? Are there visible teeth problems for the cat? It can be quite difficult to see if there is something wrong with the cat's throat, mainly because they are not used to having their tongues out and saying 'ahhh'. This examination needs an ophthalmoscope.

- Palpitation of the lymph nodes: Are they visibly enlarged or painful?

- Listening to lungs and heart using the stethoscope: Is there something unusual for breath sounds, heart rhythm, or a heart murmur? The auscultation will be done on both sides of the cat's chest.
- Palpitation of your Wegie's abdomen: Is the cat acting weirdly, seems uncomfortable, or palpable abnormalities?

- Seeing the thyroid glands: Are they enlarged?

WHAT IS THE ORDER OF THE EXAMINATION?

Chapter Nine: Keeping Your Norwegian Foreign Cats Healthy and Safe

Vets like to perform the examination in their won ways, especially with the parts that they are examining. It does not matter where they begin, as long as they will examine everything. Remember, this vet examination is done every time you go to the vet.

WHAT CAN I DO TO HELP DURING THE VET EXAMINATION?

You need to be quiet during the course of your Norwegian Forest Cat's physical examination, especially when the vet is using a stethoscope. Talking during the examination will lead to interruption of your vet's concentration and could interfere with the thoroughness. You can ask questions and suggestions after the cat's examination.

WHAT CAN I ASK MY VET?

- Do I need to examine my cat at home daily?
- What do I need to look for?
- Do you think my cat is underweight, overweight, or just right?
- Are there any problems with my cat?
- What is the way to change or remove the problem?

Chapter Nine: Keeping Your Norwegian Foreign Cats Healthy and Safe

Even if you are pretty precautious with everything, sometimes, your cat will still be sick. However, you can still treat some health problems if you spot early signs, you can give prompt treatment for any condition it may have. Here are the common cat health problems that your cat may encounter once or twice in its lifetime:

LOWER URINARY TRACT DISEASE

Feline Lower Urinary Tract Disease, or the FLUTD, has a lot of conditions that can affect your cat's urethra and bladder. The symptoms for this disease are not using the litter box, straining even if not producing urine. Aside from this, your cat may also excessively lick its genital area, and there is blood present in the urine. If you ever see these symptoms, make sure to contact your vet immediately.

This could be a painful sign of urethral blockage, which could be fatal in the long run. The major culprit for this disease is infection, cancer, bladder stones, and urinary tract blockage. The treatment for this disease will involve antibiotics, removal of the blockage, and pain medication. Your vet may even suggest a change of diet and increase of water intake to prevent other problems.

Chapter Nine: Keeping Your Norwegian Foreign Cats Healthy and Safe

INFECTIOUS DISEASE

The most common infection that your cat will have involves its respiratory system. The symptoms usually involve teary eyes, cough, and sores in the mouth, runny nose, sneezing, or coughing.

The main treatment for this infection is not really known now. However, you still need to have an evaluation for your cat because this disease could be fatal. Another common infectious disease is the feline panleukopenia, this is a highly contagious viral illness that is caused by the feline parvovirus.

The symptoms include fever, loss of appetite, dehydration, bloody diarrhea, and lethargy. Just like the above disease, there is no known medication that could kill the virus; however, the treatment will include drinking lots of fluid and watching your cat's overall health to see if your cat can fight off the infection on its own.

If your cat is just under eight weeks of age, there is only a little chance of survival, so you need to have the cat vaccine against the feline panleukopenia.

CANCER

Chapter Nine: Keeping Your Norwegian Foreign Cats Healthy and Safe

The most common type of cat cancer is the lymphosarcoma or the cancer in the lymph system that is known to be associated with the feline leukemia virus. The origin is said to be in the chest or in the intestine.

Another kind of cancer that can be found in your cat is squamous cell carcinoma, especially the white ones. The treatment for this disease heavily depends on the stage and type of cancer, which may include chemotherapy, surgery, immunotherapy, and even radiation. You need to find a vet who specializes in oncology to treat your cat's cancer.

HEARTWORM DISEASE

This is quite a tricky disease, as some cats will not show any symptoms while some may show signs such as coughing, vomiting, and respiratory problems. Unfortunately, there is no safe and effective treatment for heartworm, which could also be fatal. Some cats may fight this off.

In some severe cases, your vet will recommend medications that will reduce the inflammatory response or even surgery to remove heartworm. The process is very risky.

Chapter Nine: Keeping Your Norwegian Foreign Cats Healthy and Safe

FLEAS

Fleas are very common disease of your cat. These are parasites that will feed of the blood of your pet. Some early signs that your cat has fleas are hair loss, scratching, and bald patches, especially to those places where your cat has licked excessively.

You may also see the flea eggs, fleas, or flea excretion in your Norwegian Forest Cat's fur. The treatment to stop this problem is applying a product specially designed to kill fleas and prevent egg development. You need to be sure that you use flea - control products that are especially designed for cats, not those for dogs. Remember, cats are very sensitive to insecticide and a wrong product could potentially kill your beloved Norwegian Forest Cat.

KIDNEY DISEASE

Kidney disease could potentially attack your cat through reducing the ability to excrete their waste in the urine; this could lead to dangerous toxin build up in the bloodstream.

This disease could be caused by the following: exposure to toxins, kidney stone, high blood pressure,

Chapter Nine: Keeping Your Norwegian Foreign Cats Healthy and Safe

infection, and even cancer. Your cat's age is another great factor in developing this disease, older cat gets this disease more.

Symptoms for this disease includes weight loss, lethargy, decrease in appetite, and vomiting or diarrhea. However, some cats do not show the symptoms at all. The initial treatment for this disease knows what cause of the kidney disease is then treating the sickness. In some severe cases, your cat may need to undergo kidney transplant or dialysis.

DENTAL PROBLEMS

Some symptoms for your cat's dental disease will often involve difficulty in eating, change in chewing hait, and even bad breath.

Your cat's bad breath will indicate digestive problems or gingivitis. Other signs of the problem will involve discoloration, red or swollen gums, ulcer on the tongue or gums, loose teeth, constant pawing at the mouth area, and excessive drooling. These things could affect your cat greatly.

If you think your cat has dental problems, you need to take it the vet dentist immediately. He or she will suggest good oral hygiene, brushing the cat's teeth with a toothbrush and toothpaste that is especially made for cats, and giving a new chew toy for exercising, and removing tartar before it hardens up.

FRACTURES

Contrary from the popular myth, cats can and will get hurt especially when they fall of one or two storey windows. The short distance of the fall can't give them a chance to adjust their bodies that will enable them to fall correctly.

Some signs that your cat might have fallen off a window are not moving and even limping. If you see your cat falling off a window, you need to rush it to the vet, or animal hospital immediately. Your cat can survive only if you have it treated immediately.

DIARRHEA AND VOMITING

These two illnesses is commonly associated with the things that they have eaten. This could be from the food that they have eaten, or the plan that did not agree with their body system, or even eating too quickly. These could be a sign of some even serious illness or even infection.

Chapter Nine: Keeping Your Norwegian Foreign Cats Healthy and Safe

If the diarrhea or vomiting only occurred once, this is not usually a cause for your concern. However, if you see your cat having multiple episodes over a couple of days, take your cat to your vet immediately.

The treatment for this disease usually includes giving fluids to fight against dehydration and not feeding your cat for a period of 12 to 24 hours. This action will be followed by a bland diet that consists of boiled potato, boneless chicken, or cooked rice. Ask your vet for medications immediately.

OBESITY

This is a common cat health issue that cats face today; this will include a number of ailments such as liver problems, joint pain, and diabetes.

You should be able to feel your Norwegian Forest Cat's ribs and backbones without pressing too hard, especially those with a healthy diet. Aside from this, you can see a discernible waist between the hips and lower ribs. When you view the cat from the side, you should see the tuck in between the tummy, lower ribs, and hips.

Chapter Nine: Keeping Your Norwegian Foreign Cats Healthy and Safe

These are just some of the common diseases that your cat may face over the course of their life. Be aware and make sure you know the signs that may affect your cat's health. Knowing these things will arm you with enough knowledge on what to do next when these things happen.

The Norwegian Forest Cat in General

     We have thoroughly discussed all about our dearest Norwegian Forest Cat. It is one hell of a ride, now, it is time to wrap things up and summarize everything that we have learned. This chapter will give us an overview of everything that we have learned about the Norwegian Forest Cat. These are vital information to help you in taking care of your beloved Wegie. There are still a lot of information left for you to learn, you can search up more info through the internet and other resources.

Put your knowledge to the test and buy your very first Norwegian Forest Cat today! Enjoy spending time with your fur buddy!

Norwegian Forest Cat's Basic Info

Origin: Norway

Breed Size: medium size

Body Type and Appearance: they have a well-balanced body structure, with great emerald green eyes (with specks of gold), and an equilateral triangular shape of a head.

Height: 48 inches (122 cm)

Weight: 22 lbs (10 kg)

Group: Longhair

Coat Length: double coat, dense and long

Coat Texture: smooth and firm

Color: golden, fawn, black, brown, white

Temperament: kind, gentle, loving, cat with a strong nurturing instinct.

Strangers: they hide under furniture or even hide in another room

Other Cats: gets along well with other cat

Other Pets: they are friendly with other pets

Health Conditions: generally healthy but may contract several diseases such as hip dysplasia, glycogen storage disease, and hypertrophic cardiomyopathy.

Lifespan: average 12 to 16 years

Legal Requirements and Cat Licensing:

United States: Cat licensing is regulated at state level, there is no underlying rule for federal requirement.

United Kingdom: Special permits are needed if you want to travel with your pet. But, you may still need to quarantine your pet.

Other countries: Prepare the necessary documents during your travel. The documents are the rabies certificate, vaccinations. Aside from these, research on the other requirements needed by the country.

Purchasing and Selecting a Healthy Breed

Where to Purchase: Online Stores, Backyard/Private Breeders, Cat Conventions or Pet Conferences

Characteristics of a Reputable Breeder: There are many telltale signs of a reputable breeder. A major telltale sign is asking you about your preference. The breeder would want its pet to go to a happy and healthy family. Aside from this, s/he can answer your questions easily.

Characteristics of a Healthy Breed: You need to get up close to the pet and see for the tell-tale signs of good health. Start from the eyes, up to its tail. Make sure that it looks overall healthy. Do not look at the cat if it is just "cute"! Make sure it can socialize with the other litter easily.

Habitat Requirements for Norwegian Forest Cats: Provide enough space for your pet. It should have its own quiet and private place for it to stay. Aside from this, give an appropriate play area and scratching post for your pet.

Housing Temperature: the normal house temperature should be just right, not too cold nor too hot.

Nutrition and Food

Norwegian Forest Cats need a lot of nutrients to ensure that it will grow up healthy. You can give diverse food so your cat may choose its own preference, aside from this; your cat will be able to gain a lot of nutrients and vitamins from this endeavour.

How to Feed Your Cat: There are a lot of techniques for you to feed your cat. You may want to consult your vet on the best way possible. Be open to all the options to know how to feed your cat easily.

Feeding Amount/Frequency: There are a lot of factors to consider when you feed your cat. First, you need to know how old is your cat, are there restrictions for it, and is it overall healthy. Knowing these things is important for you and your cat's overall health.

Grooming and Training Your Norwegian Forest Cat

How to Brush Your Cat's Teeth: Brush your cat's teeth daily, if it cannot, you can do it twice a week first.

How to Trim Your Cat's Nails: Trim your cat's nail once a week or twice a month. You may need to practice this habit first, though.

Cleaning Your Cat's Ears: Remove the normal wax buildup using a cat ear cleaning solution and squeeze a few drops in the ear canal. However, you just do this occasionally.

It is still ideal to clean your cat's ears occasionally just to

Showing Your Norwegian Forest Cats:

- Must appear enthusiastic, lively and active
- Must be a colorful cat with a ticked coat
- Must be medium – size
- Should show a hard and muscular body structure

- Should be physically, and temperamentally well - balanced
- Must have passed the specific requirements of the breed standard.

(Look up Breed Standard in Chapter 7 for complete list)

Breeding Your Norwegian Cats

Gestation Period: 65 to 67 days or around 6 weeks

Litter Size: Norwegian Forest cats typically give birth to 6 kittens on average and up to a maximum of 12 kittens

Maturity: They become fully mature at around five years

Recommended Vaccinations:

- ✓ Rabies
- ✓ Feline Leukemia
- ✓ Chlamydophila
- ✓ Calicivirus
- ✓ Feline Infectious Peritonitis
- ✓ Bordetella
- ✓ Giardia
- ✓ Panleukopenia
- ✓ Rhinotracheitis
    - ✓ Feline Immunodeficiency Virus

Glossary of Cat Terms

Abundism – Referring to a cat that has markings more prolific than is normal.

Acariasis – A type of mite infection.

ACF – Australian Cat Federation

Affix – A cattery name that follows the cat's registered name; cattery owner, not the breeder of the cat.

Agouti – A type of natural coloring pattern in which individual hairs have bands of light and dark coloring.

Ailurophile – A person who loves cats.

Albino – A type of genetic mutation which results in little to no pigmentation, in the eyes, skin, and coat.

Allbreed – Referring to a show that accepts all breeds or a judge who is qualified to judge all breeds.

Alley Cat – A non-pedigreed cat.

Alter – A desexed cat; a male cat that has been neutered or a female that has been spayed.

Amino Acid – The building blocks of protein; there are 22 types for cats, 11 of which can be synthesized and 11 which must come from the diet (see essential amino acid).

Anestrus – The period between estrus cycles in a female cat.

Any Other Variety (AOV) – A registered cat that doesn't conform to the breed standard.

ASH – American Shorthair, a breed of cat.

Back Cross – A type of breeding in which the offspring is mated back to the parent.

Balance – Referring to the cat's structure; proportional in accordance with the breed standard.

Barring – Describing the tabby's striped markings.

Base Color – The color of the coat.

Bicolor – A cat with patched color and white.

Blaze – A white coloring on the face, usually in the shape of an inverted V.

Bloodline – The pedigree of the cat.

Brindle – A type of coloring, a brownish or tawny coat with streaks of another color.

Castration – The surgical removal of a male cat's testicles.

Cat Show – An event where cats are shown and judged.

Cattery – A registered cat breeder; also, a place where cats may be boarded.

CFA – The Cat Fanciers Association.

Cobby – A compact body type.

Colony – A group of cats living wild outside.

Color Point – A type of coat pattern that is controlled by color point alleles; pigmentation on the tail, legs, face, and ears with an ivory or white coat.

Colostrum – The first milk produced by a lactating female; contains vital nutrients and antibodies.

Conformation – The degree to which a pedigreed cat adheres to the breed standard.

Cross Breed – The offspring produced by mating two distinct breeds.

Dam – The female parent.

Declawing – The surgical removal of the cat's claw and first toe joint.

Developed Breed – A breed that was developed through selective breeding and crossing with established breeds.

Down Hairs – The short, fine hairs closest to the body which keep the cat warm.

DSH – Domestic Shorthair.

Estrus – The reproductive cycle in female cats during which she becomes fertile and receptive to mating.

Fading Kitten Syndrome – Kittens that die within the first two weeks after birth; the cause is generally unknown.

Feral – A wild, untamed cat of domestic descent.

Gestation – Pregnancy; the period during which the fetuses develop in the female's uterus.

Guard Hairs – Coarse, outer hairs on the coat.

Harlequin – A type of coloring in which there are van markings of any color with the addition of small patches of the same color on the legs and body.

Inbreeding – The breeding of related cats within a closed group or breed.

Kibble – Another name for dry cat food.

Lilac – A type of coat color that is pale pinkish-gray.

Line – The pedigree of ancestors; family tree.

Litter – The name given to a group of kittens born at the same time from a single female.

Mask – A type of coloring seen on the face in some breeds.

Matts – Knots or tangles in the cat's fur.

Mittens – White markings on the feet of a cat.

Moggie – Another name for a mixed breed cat.

Mutation – A change in the DNA of a cell.

Muzzle – The nose and jaws of an animal.

Natural Breed – A breed that developed without selective breeding or the assistance of humans.

Neutering – Desexing a male cat.

Open Show – A show in which spectators are allowed to view the judging.

Pads – The thick skin on the bottom of the feet.

Particolor – A type of coloration in which there are markings of two or more distinct colors.

Patched – A type of coloration in which there is any solid color, tabby, or tortoiseshell color plus white.

Pedigree – A purebred cat; the cat's papers showing its family history.

Pet Quality – A cat that is not deemed of high enough standard to be shown or bred.

Piebald – A cat with white patches of fur.

Points – Also color points; markings of contrasting color on the face, ears, legs, and tail.

Pricked – Referring to ears that sit upright.

Purebred – A pedigreed cat.

Queen – An intact female cat.

Roman Nose – A type of nose shape with a bump or arch.

Scruff – The loose skin on the back of a cat's neck.

Selective Breeding – A method of modifying or improving a breed by choosing cats with desirable traits.

Senior – A cat that is more than 5 but less than 7 years old.

Sire – The male parent of a cat.

Solid – Also self; a cat with a single coat color.

Spay – Desexing a female cat.

Stud – An intact male cat.

Tabby – A type of coat pattern consisting of a contrasting color over a ground color.

Tom Cat – An intact male cat.

Tortoiseshell – A type of coat pattern consisting of a mosaic of red or cream and another base color.

Tri-Color – A type of coat pattern consisting of three distinct colors in the coat.

Tuxedo – A black and white cat.

Unaltered – A cat that has not been desexed.

Index

A

amino acid	107
antibodies	109

B

body	109, 110
breed	108, 109, 110, 111, 112
breeder	107, 108
breeding	108, 109, 110, 111

C

Cat Fanciers Association	109
cattery	107
CFA	109
claw	109
coat	107, 108, 109, 110, 112
color	108, 109, 110, 111, 112
cycle	110

D

desexed	107, 112
diet	107
DNA	111
domestic	110

E

ears	109, 111
essential	107

estrus 108

F

face 108, 109, 110, 111
family 110, 111
feet 110, 111
female 107, 108, 109, 110, 112
fertile 110
food 110
fur 110, 111

G

genetic 107

I

infection 107
intact 112

J

judge 107

K

kittens 110

L

lactating 109

M

male	107, 108, 111, 112
markings	107, 108, 110, 111
milk	109
mite	107
mutation	107

N

neutered	107
nose	111, 112
nutrients	109

O

offspring	108, 109

P

pattern	107, 109, 112
pedigree	108, 110
pigmentation	107, 109
protein	107
purebred	111

S

show	107, 111
skin	107, 111, 112
standard	108, 109, 111

T

tail	109, 111
traits	112

Photo Credits

Page 1 Photo by user Gunnar Þór Gunnarsson via Flickr.com,

https://www.flickr.com/photos/gunnsi/430456132/

Page 4 Photo by user ccho via Flickr.com,

https://www.flickr.com/photos/ccho/6375391567/

Page 13 Photo by user Stuart via Flickr.com,

https://www.flickr.com/photos/silverfox09/3483793872/

Page 32 Photo by user Ed Clayton via Flickr.com,

https://www.flickr.com/photos/edclayton/4857994646/

Page 42 Photo by user Dick Smit via Flickr.com,

https://www.flickr.com/photos/froskeland/2120971155/

Page 50 Photo by user Airflore via Flickr.com,

https://www.flickr.com/photos/froskeland/2120971155/

Page 59 Photo by user Dick Smit via Flickr.com,

https://www.flickr.com/photos/froskeland/6013952056/

Page 66 Photo by user Mycatkins via Flickr.com,

https://www.flickr.com/photos/bigmikeyeah/9372382560/

Page 74 Photo by user Dick Smit via Flickr.com, https://www.flickr.com/photos/froskeland/1924143328/

Page 84 Photo by user Melissa Sundman via Flickr.com, https://www.flickr.com/photos/105677693@N05/10411657815/

Page 99 Photo by user PCB75 via Flickr.com, https://www.flickr.com/photos/ainhoap/396978662/

References

Norwegian Forest Cat – Vetstreet.com

http://www.vetstreet.com/cats/norwegian-forest-cat#0_xx71q37z

About the Norwegian Forest Cat – Cat Fanciers Organization

http://cfa.org/Breeds/BreedsKthruR/NorwegianForestCat.aspx

Norwegian Forest Cat – Cattime.com

http://cattime.com/cat-breeds/norwegian-forest-cats#/slide/1

Cat Equipment Basics: What You Need – Vetbabble.com

https://www.vetbabble.com/cats/getting-started-cats/cat-equipment-basics/

What are the Benefits of Having a Kitten? – TheNest.com

https://pets.thenest.com/benefits-having-kitten-6429.html

Choosing A Cat Or Kitten: Which Is Better For You? – Dummies.Com

http://www.dummies.com/pets/cats/cat-adoption/choosing-a-cat-or-kitten-which-is-better-for-you/

How to Choose a Breed and Find a Good Cat Breeder – ProfessorsHouse.com https://www.professorshouse.com/how-to-choose-a-breed-and-find-a-good-cat-breeder/

Pros and Cons of Owning a Cat – PetHelpful.com

https://pethelpful.com/cats/Pros-and-Cons-of-Owning-a-Cat

Living Spaces for Cats - Ctsanimals.ca

http://www.ctsanimals.ca/va1040/com/assets/data/pdf/kennel/needToKnow4c_10.pdf

11 Tips for Cat-Proofing Your Home this Fall – Catster.com

http://www.catster.com/lifestyle/how-to-cat-proof-your-home

Your Cat's Nutritional Needs: The Basics – Feline – Nutrition.org

https://feline-nutrition.org/nutrition/your-cats-nutritional-needs-the-basics

How To Choose The Right Food For Your Cat - TheCatSite.com

https://thecatsite.com/ams/how-to-choose-the-right-food-for-your-cat.29707/

Different Types of Healthy Cat Food – PurrsNGrrs.com

http://purrsngrrs.com/different-types-of-cat-food/

How Often Should You Feed Your Cat? – Cornell.edu

https://www2.vet.cornell.edu/departments-centers-and-institutes/cornell-feline-health-center/health-information/feline-health-topics/how-often-should-you-feed-your-cat

What not to feed your cat – Vets – Now.com

https://www.vets-now.com/2017/02/foods-poisonous-to-cats/

The Five Essential Cat Grooming Tools – Catster.com

http://www.catster.com/cat-grooming/cat-grooming-tools

Basic Cat Training Tips – VetBabble.com

https://www.vetbabble.com/cats/behavior-and-training/basic-cat-training/

Cat Grooming – WebMD.com

https://pets.webmd.com/cats/guide/cat-grooming#1

A Thorough Cat Checkup: What to Expect and How You Can Help -PetHealthNetwork.com

http://www.pethealthnetwork.com/cat-health/cat-checkups-preventive-care/a-thorough-cat-checkup-what-expect-and-how-you-can-help

The Top 10 Cat Health Problems - EverydayHealth.com

https://www.everydayhealth.com/pet-health/common-cat-health-problems.aspx

10 Reasons Norwegian Forest Cats are Great for Families - KittenToob.com

https://kittentoob.com/cat-breeds/10-reasons-norwegian-forest-cats-great-families/

4 Tips for Moving Overseas with Pets - TransitionsAbroad.com

http://www.transitionsabroad.com/tazine/0810/moving-overseas-with-pets.shtml

Fun Facts about Norwegian Forest Cats – Mercola.com

https://healthypets.mercola.com/sites/healthypets/archive/2016/11/24/norwegian-forest-cat.aspx

Feeding Baby
Cynthia Cherry
978-1941070000

Axolotl
Lolly Brown
978-0989658430

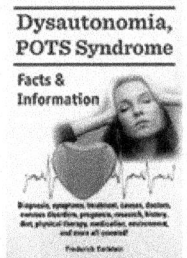

Dysautonomia, POTS Syndrome
Frederick Earlstein
978-0989658485

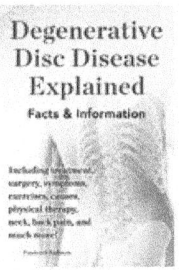

Degenerative Disc Disease Explained
Frederick Earlstein
978-0989658485

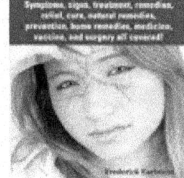

Sinusitis, Hay Fever,
Allergic Rhinitis Explained
Frederick Earlstein
978-1941070024

Wicca
Riley Star
978-1941070130

Zombie Apocalypse
Rex Cutty
978-1941070154

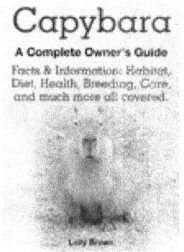

Capybara
Lolly Brown
978-1941070062

Eels As Pets
Lolly Brown
978-1941070167

Scabies and Lice Explained
Frederick Earlstein
978-1941070017

Saltwater Fish As Pets
Lolly Brown
978-0989658461

Torticollis Explained
Frederick Earlstein
978-1941070055

Kennel Cough
Lolly Brown
978-0989658409

Physiotherapist, Physical Therapist
Christopher Wright
978-0989658492

Rats, Mice, and Dormice As Pets
Lolly Brown
978-1941070079

Wallaby and Wallaroo Care
Lolly Brown
978-1941070031

Bodybuilding Supplements
Explained
Jon Shelton
978-1941070239

Demonology
Riley Star
978-19401070314

Pigeon Racing
Lolly Brown
978-1941070307

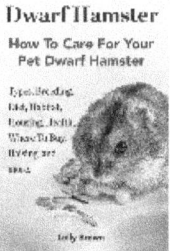

Dwarf Hamster
Lolly Brown
978-1941070390

Cryptozoology
Rex Cutty
978-1941070406

Eye Strain
Frederick Earlstein
978-1941070369

Inez The Miniature Elephant
Asher Ray
978-1941070353

Vampire Apocalypse
Rex Cutty
978-1941070321

www.ingramcontent.com/pod-product-compliance
Lightning Source LLC
Chambersburg PA
CBHW060838050426
42453CB00008B/733